# ANASAZI SUNRISE
## The Mystery of Sacrifice Rock

Copyright © 1992  by Stephen Preacher

First Edition

Published by **The Rugged Individualist**
Box 2565  El Cajon, California  92019

ISBN  1-881553-01-9

Library of Congress Catalog Card Number: 92-90872

Photography:  Ronda Preacher
Line drawing:  Brian Eddery
Cover graphics:  Ted Hansen Design Associates
Production assistance:  Joe Pearson

Printed in the United States of America

# ANASAZI SUNRISE
## The Mystery of Sacrifice Rock

Zion Canyon's
Ancient Observatory

Stephen Preacher

**The Rugged Individualist**
El Cajon, California

## Ancient Symbols

A common error of observers when first beholding ancient symbols like the petroglyphs at Sacrifice Rock is to assume that, because the glyphs seem crude in execution, the thinking behind them is also unrefined. But symbols may be representational, conceptual or arbitrary in nature. The very creation and use of petroglyphs to express an idea is indicative of analytical skills. One need only play the game of PICTIONARY to get a sense of the complexity of symbol communication.

Ted Hansen

Ted Hansen Design Associates
San Diego, California

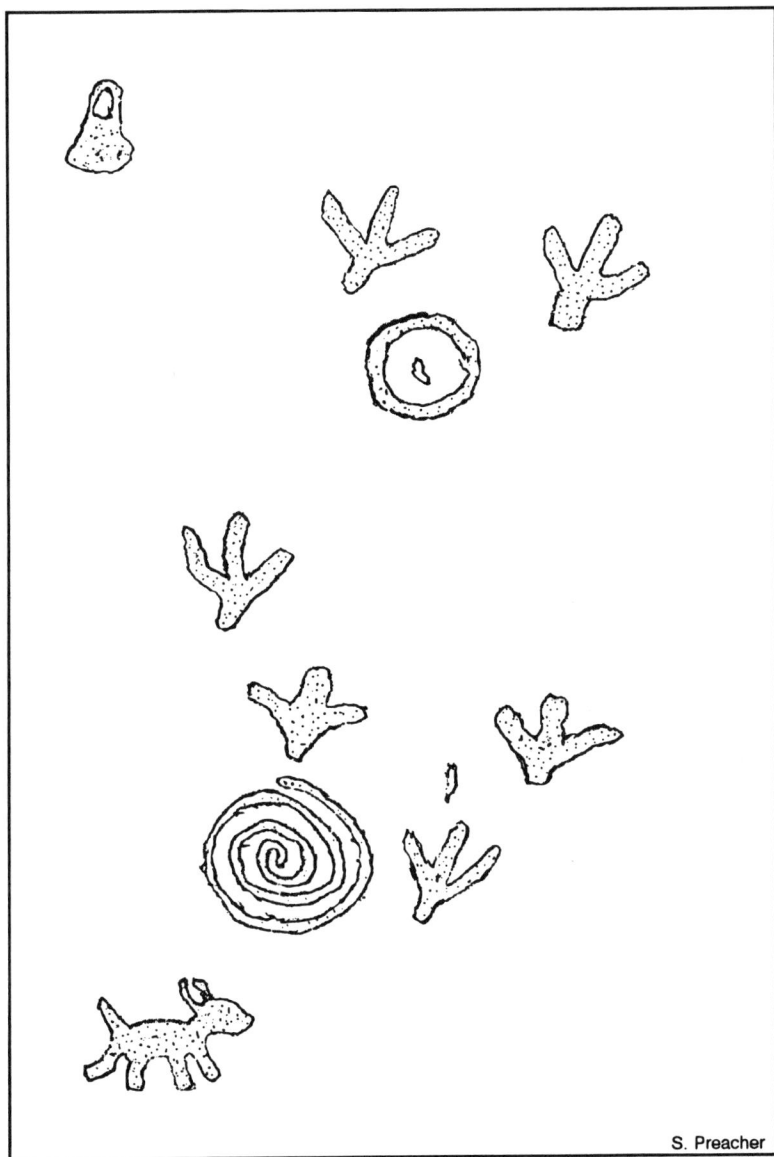

S. Preacher

The Petroglyphs

**Sacrifice Rock**
Zion National Park, Utah

# CONTENTS

*To Dad, for your inspiration to be versatile.*

*And, of course, to Ronda, Ryan and Reagan -- who make it all worthwhile.*

## Acknowledgements

A special thanks to Ronda, my wife, for patiently enduring my inattention to domestic responsibilities while writing this book, and for her assistance with many details related to it; to Ryan and Reagan, who would have preferred me to go hiking with them on Saturdays; to Connie Gale for offering great editorial suggestions while scrutinizing the text; to Ted Hansen, who generously offered a variety of helpful insights; to Art Fleming, who asked and answered pertinent questions; and to Joe Pearson, who is a wizard with computer applications. Finally, I want to thank Chuck McDowell, who taught me that a rabbit trail can lead to the most unexpected places.

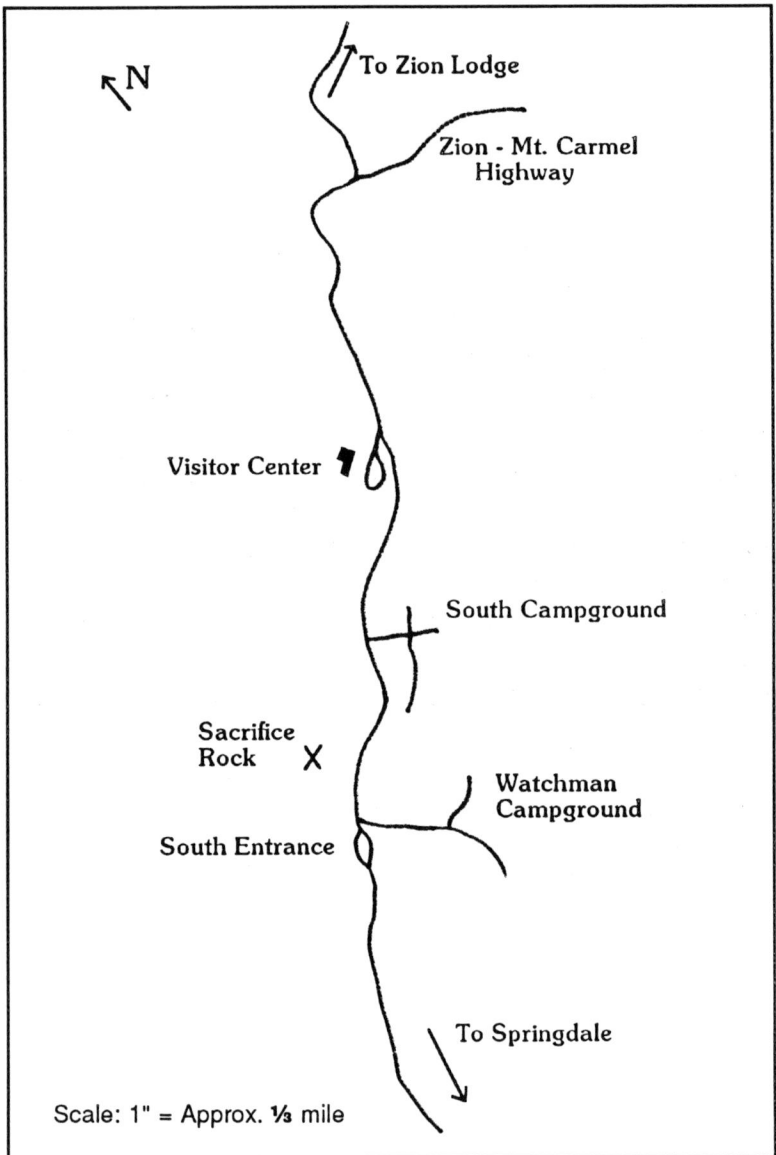

N

To Zion Lodge

Zion - Mt. Carmel
Highway

Visitor Center

South Campground

Sacrifice
Rock          X

Watchman
Campground

South Entrance

To Springdale

Scale: 1" = Approx. ⅓ mile

**Map to Sacrifice Rock**
Zion National Park, Utah

x

# Introduction

Well over a thousand years ago, the Anasazi Indians were able to record a 365 day solar year by accurately tracking the progress of the sun. But these efforts were not motivated simply by practicality. Ancient man worshiped the celestial spheres, and carefully sought the favor of the gods. Sometimes, he trembled in awe at what he beheld.

Just inside the South Entrance of Zion National Park, Utah, stands Sacrifice Rock. This monumental stone, bearing ancient symbols called petroglyphs, was previously thought to be unremarkable. But at sunrise on the day of the summer solstice, a brief but extraordinary phenomenon occurs.

As the sun breaks over the rim of Zion Canyon, a shadow appears on the face of the megalith. Like the phantom image of a howling coyote, it slowly glides down the stone panel, moving across the mysterious symbols. At the climax, the shadow precisely engulfs a spiral etching, marking the longest day of the year.

Until now, there seemed little reason to pay much notice to Sacrifice Rock. Other than the park rangers, very few people even know it has a name. The purpose of this book, therefore, is to explain its function as an ancient Anasazi observatory, worthy of recognition as a unique national treasure.

## SUNRISE

The early morning air was cool and crisp.  By 5:00 a.m. first light was already causing the sky over Zion Canyon to glow with shades of peach and aqua.  It was June 21, the day of the summer solstice, and I had waited nearly a year for this sunrise.  My wife and I hurried to get dressed, while our two boys, Ryan and Reagan, still slept soundly.

Camera equipment, shoes and bags were on the floor, making it difficult for us to maneuver around each other within the small confines of our travel trailer parked in the Watchman campground.  I could only guess how much longer it would be before the sun's rays would spill onto the canyon floor striking the face of Sacrifice Rock. If we were too late, the main quest of the trip would be lost.

I quickly lit the stovetop burner to start the small coffee percolator, hoping the strong brew would help punch me awake.  I had slept fitfully through the night, uneasy at the possibility that somehow the new alarm clock would fail to awaken me.  Sitting on the edge of the dinette, now folded down for Ryan's bed, I began to reflect on the events that led up to this moment.

In the summer of 1990, my brother, Brooks, and I had first visited Zion National Park on an extended camping tour of the Southwest. On July 4, as the temperature climbed steadily to over 100 degrees, we set up our tent in the South campground. As soon as that task was completed, we ventured into the park's Visitor Center for an air-conditioned respite from the sweltering heat.

Knowing this canyon had been inhabited more that a thousand years earlier by Anasazi Indians, I wanted to see what traces of their society still remained. Some of the most durable evidence left by these prehistoric people was in the form of petroglyphs--images and symbols pecked or carved in stone. In addition, there were a few sheltered places where  pictographs, or painted images, still remained in certain areas of the Southwest.

At the Visitor Center, I asked a ranger if there were any easily visible petroglyphs nearby.  He said there was nothing really significant in that area of the park, but suggested that I might visit a spot near the South Entrance.  There, not far from the road, I would find some simple and rather unremarkable petroglyphs among some large boulders. Regretfully, he said, the site had been vandalized. When asked if anyone had attempted to interpret the ancient rock art, he assured me that the meaning of the symbols was "anybody's guess."

Brooks and I decided to look for the petroglyphs, but as we drove along examining the jumbled rocks, we were unable to pinpoint anything that seemed to fit the description.

Shortly we found ourselves near the gatehouse at the South Entrance, asking directions from another ranger, who was collecting entrance fees from the new visitors.

We were directed to park the car at a nearby pull-out and to look for a small footpath winding through the brush. The path would lead to a tall, flat-sided sandstone formation standing slightly apart from the other large stones. Following the directions, we realized the area was clearly visible, once we knew what to look for.

Pecked into the surface of the rock panel was a small spiral, some bird feet, and a four-legged creature--perhaps a mountain sheep, dog or coyote. At first glance, it seemed that the ranger back at the Visitor Center had been right. Certainly the petroglyphs were not remarkable works of primitive art. I even wondered if maybe the Indian artist had used this location as an opportunity to sharpen his skills.

Unfortunately, the smooth vertical panel had provided some thoughtless park visitors the tempting opportunity to scratch lines and make other weak attempts to leave messages, amounting to nothing more than unsightly defacement. Later, I learned this was allegedly the reason why park officials called the site Sacrifice Rock.

The place gave me an unsettled feeling that this was more than just a big rock with a conveniently flat surface on which to leave messages. Boulders with flattened sides were plentiful throughout the canyon. There was something else here, something remarkable about the commanding presence of the enormous megalithic stone.

Could this place have held a religious significance to the ancient Anasazi Indians who had lived in this magnificent canyon? Perhaps the huge stone generated some sense of mystical awe, some magnetic compelling force that struck to the core of imagination. I tried to recall how other monolithic structures had played a role in the religion of ancient civilizations. Intruding upon those thoughts, scenes of the monolith in the movie "2001" played through my mind.

While examining the large stones, their orientation captured my attention. The whole configuration faces due east. And the huge wedge-shaped slab, propped at an angle in front of the megalith, reminded me of the shadow marker on a sundial. What if the wedge did indeed cast some sort of shadow on the panel behind it?

Looking back at the spiral, I was reminded of the Anasazi sun calendar discovered in 1977 at Chaco Canyon, New Mexico. High atop Fajada Butte, a spiral petroglyph is split through the center by a shaft of light called a "sun dagger." The phenomenon occurs on June 21, marking the summer solstice and longest day of the year.

On the megalith behind me was also a spiral. But spirals are found among petroglyphs all over the Southwest. Hovenweep National Monument had the only other spiral I could think of that had any solar phenomenon associated with it. Still, I

5

wondered if something like that might happen here. At length, my brother and I left the site, but thoughts of it continued to nag at me throughout the afternoon.

With a growing suspicion about the significance of the megalith and its symbols, I returned to the site the next morning, July 5. The hot clear sky of the day before had given way to a heavy overcast. A storm was brewing. The sun was obscured by the clouds, but its smeary glow was hanging low over Bridge Mountain, which formed part of the east rim of the canyon.

I positioned myself between the spiral and the large angular wedge, and sighted a line toward Bridge Mountain. The brighter area of clouds marking the sun's position was just a few degrees to the north of being directly in line with the pointed tip of the slab and the spiral.

Adjusting for where I thought the sun would have risen on June 21, it seemed highly probable that the wedge could indeed cast a shadow to slice through the center of the spiral on the morning of the solstice. Such a phenomenon would occur with exact precision only once a year.

If my hypothesis proved to be true, Sacrifice Rock would hold one of the few remaining, fully intact sun calendars known to exist. Certainly it would be the one most easily accessible to the general American public. And what a bonus to have it fall under the protection of a Zion National Park, and the careful supervision of its rangers!

Upon returning to San Diego that summer, I shared my theories with Dr. Chuck McDowell, a professor of ancient history. As a friend and professional colleague, Chuck had sparked my interest in ancient sun calendars and solar observatories only a couple of years earlier. This continued interest led to my suspicion that the spiral at Sacrifice Rock might be more significant than anyone had guessed. I invited Chuck to return to the park with me in June, 1991, to help document the solstice phenomenon, should it occur.

Now the year had passed, and we would soon learn the answer. My reflections were interrupted by the reckless burping of the coffee pot. Its fresh aroma tugged me back into the present. Ronda tried to shake the boys awake, but was answered with grunts and groans. The anticipation we all felt the day before had kept the boys awake late into the evening, but their excitement had now given place to fatigue.

Chuck and Thressie McDowell, who had arrived shortly after we found our campsite, were able to pitch their tent next to our trailer. A look out our trailer window revealed all was still quiet within the little dome. I remembered with amusement that the McDowell's miniature poodle had shared their snug quarters throughout the night.

It had been a short night. Even while I was still burning my lips on the hot coffee, Chuck rapped sharply on the door of our trailer, urging us to make haste. Morning was breaking, and he was ready to start setting up over at the rocks.

Ronda and I finally tugged the boys out of bed and got them into their clothes. General confusion broke out as they gathered up parkas, hats and wind breakers. At last, we were ready to pile into the car for the short drive to the roadside where we would leave the vehicles.

There was a protest about breakfast, and someone threw in a box of doughnuts. I hastily grabbed the coffee pot, a backpacking stove, and the video camera. I'd charged the two batteries before leaving home and hoped they would last long enough to do the job. Once the action started there would be no turning back.

Parking our cars, we were relieved to see that Sacrifice Rock still stood in shadow. But the upper edge of the west canyon rim was already bathed in sunlight. The dark recesses and rugged sculpture of the high walls provided a breathtaking study of contrasts in color and shading. The flaming light patterns seemed to be descending slowly, and I judged there would be sufficient time to set up our video cameras and find the best positions to settle in and wait.

Thressie stationed herself on the large rock that propped the shadow wedge in position. Tucked under the overhang of its point, she balanced her camcorder on her knees to steady it. There she could begin taping while finding some shelter from the thermal wind currents generated by the warming canyon walls.

On the opposite side of the shadow wedge, out of Thressie's view, I secured my tripod just in front of what I called the "platform rock," because of its fairly level surface. This position afforded an elevated vantage point of all the petroglyphs, and a sure footing for my camcorder.

I had operated camcorders, including several different models, on various occasions over the years, and they all worked about the same way. This one was brand new, and I had used this trip as the justification to purchase it. But in all the rush of last minute preparation, I had not taken the time to become acquainted with all its features. Now I began to regret it.

Fumbling with the batteries, I practiced making a quick change to avoid losing time at perhaps a critical moment. That worked alright, but the function of some of the other buttons was not entirely clear. Procrastination had been foolish. What a waste if my unfamiliarity caused the taping to be erratic or piecemeal. I was really glad Thressie was behind that rock with her camcorder.

I removed the lens cap to adjust the camera and take some lead footage. The gusting breeze whipped the cap around by its security line, clacking it wildly against the body of the camera. I fastened it down to the hand strap, but the camera itself shook with some of the gusts. It was the first day of summer, but we were still in the cool shadows. The chilly breeze forced me to zip up my wind breaker.

The warming rays of the sun were now halfway down the canyon wall in front of me. We were finally as ready as we were going to be. The boys began to explore the surrounding area, and Ronda snapped off some still shots with the 35mm camera. I found a small niche between some of the stones to  shelter the little campstove and coffee pot from the wind. Another gulp of hot coffee would help fend off the chill.

The position and intensity of the ascending sun behind Bridge Mountain gave reassurance that a shadow would soon appear on the petroglyph panel. Chuck and I speculated about where it might first occur. I expected an angular shadow to strike fairly high above the spiral and gradually descend through its middle. Whatever was to happen couldn't take much longer. It was nearly 7:45 a.m.

Expecting a little more warning before the need to start recording, we were caught by surprise as the megalith's surface became radiant within only 45 seconds. Suddenly--like a phantom--an amazing image seemed to emerge from the darkest area of desert varnish. It appeared a third of the way up the extreme left edge of the stone's face. As the contrast grew stronger, the shadow developed an uncanny resemblance to the head of a howling coyote!

The nose of the image materialized just above a phallic symbol that had been carved into the surface. As the excitement of the moment increased, the exhilaration of discovery coursed through my veins. I began to realize that no one else beyond the six of us had any idea of what was happening here. Perhaps human eyes had not witnessed this phenomenon for a thousand years. Indeed, a glance around revealed no one else anywhere in sight.

My camcorder worked flawlessly, and I was able to leave the platform rock and approach the shadow while the taping continued. For the next hour, we tried to absorb the significance of the ancient drama unfolding before our eyes.

The entire process was captivating. As the sun rose higher, the coyote image glided down the face of the colossal stone. Slowly and almost imperceptibly it moved, with the deliberateness of the large hand on a clock dial. With exact precision, the head and throat moved into position until the edge of its contours fit against the placement of the spiral, with the eagle foot above, and the dog or coyote pecked below it. Now there was no doubt that this really was a solar calendar.

We were convinced that the spiral would mark the climax of the phenomenon when the shadow dropped through its center. But unexpectedly, the features of the coyote image began to compress, while its form started to shift to the right. It continued in this manner, covering the petroglyph until it split the snake-like spiral through the middle.

At that point, the shadow's edge touched the center and tail of the spiral at the same moment. Then the snout of the coyote continued to move to the right and down, its dimensions precisely engulfing or "swallowing" the spiral, which is about eight inches in diameter. The fit was exact.

It seemed as though the shadow paused momentarily, but then the spiral began to emerge on the left. The nose passed over the left toe of another eagle foot positioned to the right of the spiral. It then pivoted under the foot, briefly causing the three toes to appear to protrude from its tip. Finally, the elongated image slid below the glyphs.

I stood quietly in the warming sunshine. The occasional sounds of waking campers and the robust aroma of breakfast campfires drifted up the slope on the breeze. A curious passer-by, apparently seeing our cameras, started toward us, paused a few moments, then walked back toward the road and away.

A while later, a ranger slowed his car, peered up at our little group but drove off. I was very glad no one had interrupted us. At that moment, I didn't feel like sharing this with any strangers.

What a sense of awe and mystical power the Indians of this canyon must have felt. This was the stuff that gave birth to legends and substance to pagan religions.

Here, in this yet unspoiled setting, so little had changed since the Anasazi shaman or high priest must have presided over the ritual ceremony celebrating the creation and rebirth of his people, a ceremony so closely associated with the summer solstice.

How many generations had gathered in this natural amphitheater to worship the sun so long ago? Perhaps some of the traditions and ceremonies of North American Indians had their early seeds in places such as this.

I remembered that the Mayas and Aztecs worshipped the sun, as did the mound building Cahokia of Mississippi, thousands of miles from Mesoamerica. They all had three things in common: highly-sophisticated, far-reaching trade and communication networks; precise celestial calendars; and a sun god that required human sacrifice.

It seemed as if the door of the ages had been unlocked before me. Just like in the romantic imaginings of my youth, I had been transported back through time. But this feeling did not come from reading a book or standing by a lifeless museum exhibit. The thrill of this experience involved all my senses.

That morning the ancient coyote had suddenly returned in a blaze of light. It had spoken through silence. It had moved. Somehow, the age-old phantom still lived!

The clump grass and creosote bushes rustled gently in the slowing thermal currents. The others in our group began to carry their belongings back to the cars, chattering excitedly along the path. Alone, I paused to savor the setting just a few more moments, my mind reeling with questions. What might have really happened here, so very long ago?

## 2

## ANCIENT ASTRONOMERS

The sun, moon, planets and constellations have long been known to play a major role in the religions of past cultures.  Scholars are now realizing that observation of these heavenly bodies was accomplished using highly complex mathematical calculations.  As a result, a new discipline known as archaeoastronomy, has developed which studies the sophisticated astronomical skills achieved by ancient civilizations.  Research has revealed that the placement of a great number of temples and architectural structures of past civilizations had a primary relationship to the movement and alignment of celestial bodies.

Perhaps the strongest factor motivating the careful study of the celestial spheres was the worship of the sun as a god.  Religions involving sun worship were widespread throughout the ancient world, and some of the greatest structures ever built were associated with this purpose.

In early Mesopotamia, pyramidal, stepped sun temples called ziggurats were constructed.  From this region, most likely the city of Babylon, came the wise men or "magi" recorded in the account of Jesus' birth in the Bible.

These astrologers, who searched the heavens for signs foretelling the future, were not simply wealthy fortune tellers out for adventure. Rather, they were scientists and mathematicians--the intelligentsia of the ancient world--highly schooled in the patterns of celestial movement. What the magi found became the turning point of civilization.

Almost three thousand years before Christ, the technology of the Egyptians had reached such levels that their knowledge still continues to amaze modern engineers and astronomers alike. Although the pyramids were assumed to be the magnificent tombs of the pharaohs, studies have shown that they were also observatories. The central passage leading down into the Great Pyramid of Cheops, for example, was perfectly aligned with the North Star. Five thousand years ago, before the earth had shifted slightly, that star was Thuban. Today, it is Polaris.

The pyramid was also a massive timepiece. In the winter, its shadow moved across the desert floor tracking the hours, days and years. In seasonal contrast, the rays of the summer sun would reflect off the highly polished surface to continue the time-keeping process. Thus, the Egyptians could accurately predict the solar equinoxes and solstices, along with every other essential event. Science was the servant of religion, and central to their religious system was Re (or Ra), the god of the sun and all creation.

Even before the pharaohs, however, Neolithic men employed their highest technical skills--apparently motivated by reverence for the heavens. Around 3100 B.C., far away in what is now England, work was begun on another engineering marvel called Stonehenge. When completed, the structure ultimately consisted of concentric rings of massive megaliths placed in an upright position. Around 2100 B.C., stone pillars weighing about four tons each were hauled from 240 miles away.

During another phase of construction, perhaps one hundred years later, the addition of great linteled stones completed another circle. Quarried some twenty miles north of the location, these stone were about thirty feet long and weighed fifty tons each! Further modifications to the arrangement continued periodically until about 1550 B.C.

The purpose of Stonehenge has remained the subject of heated debate. It appears, however, to have been used as an observatory to track and predict the movement of celestial bodies, primarily the sun and moon. In close conjunction with that theory, it is also assumed to have been a center of religious worship, perhaps even involving human sacrifice.

Fixation on the sun as the supreme deity also played a dominant role in Indo-European religions. Again, integrating science with religion, the observation of the solar year and other celestial measures of time resulted in the origination of various calendrical devices.

The belief in the sun as the giver and sustainer of life most likely developed from its close association with warmth, light, security and, later, with the success of cultivated harvests. Wherever it was worshipped, the sun was identified as the ruler of the heavens (and usually of the underworld, as the sun completed its circuit). It was the all-seeing eye and the giver of wisdom. Over the millennia, additional mystical qualities were attributed to the sun and the other celestial bodies as well.

Some time around the birth of Christ, in the present day Nazca Valley of Peru, extensive systems of lines were etched in the surface of the terrain.   Known as the Nazca Lines, they are precisely-fashioned animal shapes, human forms, spirals and "runways."   Many were of such great size that they are not discernible from the ground. Consequently, they were not discovered until pilots flew over the area in the twentieth century.

The magnitude and precision of these designs has prompted some individuals to advance fanciful notions about extraterrestrial visitors coming to the earth in ancient times.  It has also been suggested that those visitors even brought the knowledge to engineer the great pyramids. But such views are more likely the product of our modern culture's egocentric interpretation, which sometimes fails to recognize the intellectual level and technological sophistication achieved by vanished civilizations in their own right.

John Carlson, director for the Center for Archaeoastronomy in College Park, Maryland, acknowledges that scholarly interpretations vary, but the idea of visitors from outer space is not among them.   Instead, possible explanations suggest that the Nazca Lines may be representations of constellations; the alignments of celestial bodies rising and setting; and/or possibly the connecting pathways between sacred locations. Underlying these theories is the concept that the Nazca civilization maintained a worldview which integrated earthly and celestial phenomena as a synergistic whole.

In any ancient culture, regardless of its geographic location, the complicated science of astronomy was beyond the grasp of the uneducated masses. As a highly specialized tool of divination and ritual, (along with astrology) it was usually the exclusive domain of the priesthood, and carefully guarded as such. The apparent ability to foretell the future (then as now) carried great power and influence.

Far to the north of Peru, between 1200 and 900 B.C., large earthen pyramids began to appear near the Gulf Coast of southern Mexico. This marked the rise of the Olmec culture, the first highly developed civilization in the region of Central America and Mexico, known as Mesoamerica. At about the same time, the tribal peoples who would later consolidate to form the Mayan empire had already begun to settle down (become sedentary, as the archaeologists say), cultivating corn, squash and beans.

Influenced by their Olmec predecessors, the Mayas at last began building great cities, including pyramids dedicated to the worship of the sun. The culture flourished from about A.D. 200 until about A.D. 900, ultimately reaching a population perhaps in excess of two million people.

During this Classic Period, the priestly elite developed hieroglyphic writing and an advanced system of mathematics which included the invention of zero. Their ability to calculate, combined with their meticulous observation of celestial patterns, enabled them to create a calendrical system capable of accurately predicting the dates for solar eclipses.

For the Mayas, as for the other pre-Columbian civilizations of Mesoamerica, the cycles of the sun, moon and Venus (the Morning Star), played an intimate role in the affairs of daily living. Celestial observation provided the schedule for fertility rites, planting and hunting seasons, and even the most desirable time for making war.

Knowing when to make propitiation to the gods was also essential in order to avoid great catastrophes. Bloodletting, mutilation and human sacrifice were all considered necessary and normal obligations.

The Mayan calendar included a 365 day solar calendar and a ritualistic calendar of 260 named days. This formed the operational basis for the other Mesoamerican calendars, including the calendar stone the Aztecs utilized a thousand years later. These devices also incorporated concurrent cycles of Venus and the sun into one "Calendar Round," consisting of 52 years.

Further north in the Valley of Mexico, arose the great city of Teotihuacán, "Where Men Become Gods," located about thirty miles northeast of present day Mexico City. Overlapping the Classic Period of the Mayas, the civilization based at Teotihuacán prospered from about the first century A.D. until its demise, which occurred around A.D. 750. Within that period, its population reached 200,000, and encompassed an area of eight square miles.

The Pyramid of the Sun was erected in the center of the city. Standing over two hundred feet tall, it was built on a grid matching the east-west alignments of the rising and setting sun and the constellation Pleiades. Directly under the pyramid is a natural lava cave.

The location of the pyramid is significant. It apparently depicts the belief that humankind emerged from the underworld, a theme common to the creation myths throughout the prehistoric Americas. The Pyramid of the Sun is embellished with sculptured panels having alternating representations of Quetzalcóatl, who was the Feathered Serpent, jaguars, eagles and coyotes.

Between A.D. 700 and 900, the militant Toltecs destroyed the nearly abandoned city of Teotihuacán, but continued to worship many of the same gods of its former inhabitants. This was probably because the theological worldview of the times had already widely permeated the region.

The center for the Toltec culture was the city of Tula, about fifty miles north of Mexico City. There the elite cult of Quetzalcóatl was established by its ruler, Topiltzan. He evidently commanded great power, proclaiming himself to be a god-man, the human incarnation of Quetzalcóatl, the Feathered Serpent. The concept of ruler deification was readily accepted in cultures which practiced sun worship. Quetzalcóatl's relationship with the sun was strong, and in that role, Topiltzan would have assumed direct access to the sun's power.

The process of building a new empire continued through conquest and unification of outlying tribes and villages. To assist in that effort, the Toltecs organized and strengthened the military orders of the Jaguar, Eagle and Coyote, through which they extended their influence deep into the Mayan culture of the Yucatán peninsula.

The ebb and flow of civilization continued, and Toltec domination began to collapse at the hands of hunting and gathering tribes migrating into central Mexico from the north. By the middle of the 12th century, these tribes, who collectively called themselves the Culhua-Mexica, began taking control of Mesoamerica. We know them as the Aztecs.

The Aztec society made no significant changes in the pantheon of fertility gods already established, except in terms of emphasis. Their four primary gods included Tlaloc, god of rain; Quetzalcóatl, the Feathered Serpent; Huitzilopochtli, the hummingbird and god of war; and Tonatiuh, god of the sun.

The capital city of the Aztecs was Tenochtitlán, founded in A.D. 1325 at the marshy edge of Lake Texcoco. It now rests under Mexico City. The unlikely site was chosen because the Aztec priests claimed to have received instructions from Huitzilopochtli to settle at the location where they would find an eagle perched on a cactus and eating a snake. As it turned out, this was a strategic advantage because the surrounding water made the city easily defensible for the increasingly warring Aztecs.

As with the Mayas and the Toltecs, celestial observation was essential to the survival of the Aztecs. In the fashion of their predecessors, the Aztecs tracked the pathways of the sun, stars and observable planets. All the events of their culture, religion and political economy were carefully scheduled, including war. It was with this last point that the Aztecs became entirely preoccupied. Even more belligerent than the Toltecs, they carried warfare to the extreme, making it the fundamental manifestation of their religion.

In order to ensure the survival of humanity (more realistically to extract tribute and ensure the subservience of any potential military opposition to the control of the priesthood) it was necessary to provide nourishment for the sun god, Tonatiuh. That nourishment was blood, and it was best provided by extracting and offering the still-beating heart of a sacrificial victim. Without this propitiation, the sun would go away forever, and the world would come to an end.

The Aztecs believed that some of the other gods also developed a voracious appetite for blood, and human sacrifice became the ultimate means of winning the gods' favor. When the temple of Huitzilopochtli was dedicated in 1490, accounts indicate that between 20,000 and 80,000 captives of war were sacrificed continuously over a period of four days.

Through conquest and kinship alliances, the expanding empire of the Aztecs grew to control approximately five hundred states by the early 16th century. Unification of those settlements created a land area of over 80,000 square miles with a population between five and six million.

Sustained by extensive resources, and without the aid of the wheel or beasts of burden, Tenochtitlán presided over an elaborate network of communication and mercantile trade. How could such a remarkable empire have fallen at the hands of Hernán Cortés and his band of fortune-hunting Spaniards? The answer is one of history's great ironies.

Five hundred years earlier, as the result of religious conflict, the Toltec ruler and culture hero Topiltzan-Quetzalcóatl, was driven into exile. According to one of the versions of the legend, he was transformed into Venus, the Morning Star. The story, which became widespread throughout all Mesoamerica, says that he promised he would one day return from the east. Using their sophisticated calendar, a date was set for that great occasion.

Carefully tracking the cycles of Venus and meticulously marking the days, the Aztecs, who also believed this prophecy, eagerly looked forward to Quetzalcóatl's return as the year grew closer.

Finally, messengers brought word that a group of strange bearded white men had arrived in the east. They had come from the sea, borne in crafts having white billowing wings. Furthermore, the god-men rode giant dogs and carried thunder sticks which could instantly strike down a warrior. Awe and wonder swept through the empire.

The wily Cortés, while on his quest for gold, met a coastal Indian girl who quickly made him aware of his tactical advantages. Well-versed in the traditions and prophecies of the region, the girl joined his band of soldiers as an interpreter. Learning the story of Quetzalcóatl's return, Cortés assembled an alliance of Indians and began a march toward the fabled Tenochtitlán. Passing through villages along the way, he fired up the native's hatred toward their bloodthirsty oppressors, convincing many of the villagers to join his entourage.

Watching the stars and recounting the strange omens of the times, Moctezuma waited in his capital city. Messengers came daily with wondrous gifts and strange news of the advancing god-man and his followers. The priests and all the people looked toward his arrival with great anticipation. Moctezuma would be ready for the second coming of Quetzalcóatl. He would prepare a reception proper for the gods. His calendar stone marked the year we know as 1519.

**3**

## WHO WERE THE ANASAZI?

By the time Moctezuma was at the height of his power, thousands of abandoned settlements and towns in the Southwest already stood in tomb-like silence under the blowing dust. These were once the villages of a complex culture known collectively as the Anasazi. Most of the ruins are located in the Four Corners region of southern Utah, northern Arizona, southern Colorado and northern New Mexico.

In the language of the Navajo, Anasazi means the "ancient ones," or "ancient enemies." No one knows where they came from, but the earliest evidence of the culture dates to around 700 B.C., when they can be identified as a group which probably emerged from the Desert Culture--a people who had long practiced a migratory lifestyle of foraging and hunting. Eventually, the Anasazi acquired the knowledge to become remarkably skilled basketmakers, stone masons and farmers.

The Anasazi culture has been classified into distinct periods, utilizing information which indicated an increasing complexity in the development of their civilization. The periods are currently identified as follows: Basket Maker, 100 B.C. - A.D. 500; Modified Basket Maker, 500-700; Developmental Pueblo, 700-1050; Classic Pueblo, 1050-1300; Regressive Pueblo,1300-1700; and Modern Pueblo, 1700 to the present.

As the Anasazi became more sedentary, the cultivation of corn, squash and pumpkins was enhanced using an irrigation system consisting of canals fed by reservoirs. The people advanced from living in caves, mud huts and pit houses to the building of towns and masonry structures with hundreds of rooms.

Many of their townsites included multi-storied lookout towers. Some authorities believe the towers were relay stations where long-range communication signals were flashed using mirrors, perhaps made from mica. By whatever means commerce and trade occurred, it was done without the benefit of an organized system of writing.

Towns beyond the major centers, called outliers, were linked together by hundreds of miles of arrow-straight roads that brought foot travelers from vast distances away. As with the cultures in Mesoamerica, there is no indication that the Anasazi ever used the wheel for transport purposes. Beasts of burden were also unknown.

Between A.D. 1050 and 1300, the Anasazi reached the height of their culture. By then, the art of basketmaking was surpassed by the development of exquisite pottery, a skill probably imported from Mexico. At their zenith, they built community pueblos sometimes containing 800 to 1000 rooms.

In some areas, mostly in southern Colorado, they began constructing cliff dwellings high in the recesses of canyons walls. It seems this development was motivated by the need for defense against the marauding nomadic tribes of the Apaches and Navajos. This factor, coupled with a prolonged drought during the last quarter of the 13th century, marks the end of the Classic Pueblo period.

In the later years of the culture, faced with food and wood shortages, the dwindling numbers of Anasazi began to migrate east toward the Rio Grande valley and south into Arizona. Some may have proceeded into northern Mexico to mix with the migration of people that continued further south to undermine the Toltec civilization. This movement gave rise to the origins of the Aztecs in

A.D. 1325, formally recognized by the founding of Tenochtitlán.

The Anasazi were a Nahuatl-speaking people, as were the Aztecs. Nahuatl is a branch of the Uto-Aztecan language spoken in central Mexico. It may be possible that the rapid mobilization and ascension of the Aztecs is partly due to the assimilation of some groups  of the dispersing Anasazi, whose collapsing culture already shared some elements of the Mesoamerican heritage.

There are strong indications that the Anasazi civilization, throughout its development, maintained active contact with Mesoamerica. Their religion, construction methods, and farming techniques shared numerous characteristics with their neighbors to the south.  It is also known that the trade network headquartered in Teotihuacán, central Mexico, had reached the Southwest by A.D. 700, if not well before.  Perhaps the Anasazi were an integral link in the merchant trade that spanned North America from the Pacific to the region of the present-day southeastern United States.

Mesoamerican cultural exchanges strongly influenced the development of the Temple Mound

Builders who occupied the Mississippi Valley. Archaeologists suspect that the Indians from the Yucatán regularly crossed the Gulf of Mexico in trade expeditions. On the mainland, the Anasazi would have been situated along a primary corridor of this trade loop.

By A.D. 800, probably with the aid of river transportation, merchant traders began to penetrate deep into the heartland of North America. Mesoamerican technology and religion was being widely diffused throughout the Midwest and Southeast. Great earthen mounds very similar in shape to the platform pyramids of Mesoamerica became a major characteristic of the Mississippian culture.

The largest city produced by the Mississippians was Cahokia, with a population possibly exceeding 40,000. Located in what is now East St.Louis, Illinois, a large earthen pyramid, known as Monks Mound, was built in successive stages during A.D. 900 - 1200. The mound stood 100 feet high and covered 14 acres at its base, rivaling the mass of the great pyramids constructed in Teotihuacán and Egypt.

35

Mississippian pyramid structures were utilized for several purposes, including burial mounds and platforms for the homes of the ruling aristocracy and priesthood. Pyramids were also the pattern for ceremonial temples of worship to a pantheon of gods. Similarities with Mexico were clearly reflected in Mississippian religious practices.

Evidence indicates that the practice of human sacrifice, either by strangulation or beheading, was incorporated into the religious system, along with the worship of the Feathered Serpent and the sun god. By A.D. 1200, more than a hundred years before the Aztecs had even established their first city, a death cult known as the Buzzard or Southern Cult was already prevalent in the Mississippian culture.

The cult was preoccupied with death, and evidence of its influence has appeared in numerous sites over a broad area of the Mississippi Valley. Some of the same distinctive symbols used by its followers are also found in Mesoamerica.

One of the last groups within the vanishing Mississippians, know as the Natchez, continued to engage in human sacrifice well into the 18th century. Their rulers were called Great Suns, and they were each worshipped as a deity and brother to the celestial sun itself. When a Great Sun died, wives and servants might willingly submit to strangulation so that they could accompany him on his journey.

In contrast, the Anasazi did not seem to be heavily layered with aristocratic classes or a caste system, but were instead rather egalitarian. Evidently they followed no rulers who asserted their own affiliation with deity by prescribing human offerings to appease the gods. Neither is there an indication that they were a militaristic society like the Toltecs or Aztecs, though they were familiar with the art of warfare.

Based on available information so far, the Anasazi are not known to have engaged in human sacrifice, even though the practice was contemporary with their culture and geographically widespread to the east and south. But in view of their contact with those cultures, along with the religious doctrines they shared in common, it is not unreasonable to suggest that human sacrifice may have been present, at least to a limited degree.

If they did practice the grisly ritual, however, it may have been done on a highly selective basis. Perhaps economics, limited population size, or simply a lack of hated enemies (who typically supplied the victims) would account for this.

The appreciation for life fostered in a dry and harsh environment, along with the need for each member's contribution to the success of the whole community, may have forestalled any significant trend toward human sacrifice among the Anasazi. But the environment of the culture, the religion, and the expectations associated with the practice were intact.

# 4

## INDIAN SKYWATCHERS

The Anasazi lived under the pristine skies of the desert Southwest where an awareness of the expansive heavens was ever-present. The region offered an unexcelled opportunity to observe the celestial themes which dominated their sacred beliefs. But the extent of cultural interchange with Mesoamerica was limited, and the complex stone calendars found in Mexico do not appear in the Southwest or elsewhere in North America.

Nonetheless, it is clear that nearly every North American tribe or culture group had some means of observing dates and tracking time. This was usually the responsibility of the priest or shaman. Because of the migratory lifestyle of so many groups, astronomical records and corresponding dates were probably maintained by marking on animal skins or some other lightweight and portable material.

Pictographic symbols resembling the Mesoamerican calendars very possibly may have been used by some tribes, but there is no proof of it. Contributing to the lack of tangible evidence could be the perishability of the records and the

39

likelihood that they would also have been the exclusive property of the priests. If such records of proprietary knowledge existed, they would have been considered sacred religious documents--few in number and not popularly displayed.

The contact of European explorers with North American Indians revealed little more than the ability to count days with bundles of sticks or track seasons and years by the cycles of the moon. Certainly many tribal groups, though contemporaries of one another, had remained aboriginal or in fact had regressed from higher levels of cultural and technical complexity.

In the Southwest, however, the Anasazi were attaining increasingly higher levels of technology almost until the time their culture nearly vanished. Fairly recent discoveries continue to reveal more about the degree of their achievements, a portion of which is related to the study of rock art.

Some authorities have speculated that rock art was a skill reserved for the priests and shamans. If they were the keepers of celestial timetables, they also likely would have been the ones to determine which messages would be pleasing to the gods and therefore beneficial if left to remain in stone.

Human and animal forms, spirals and bizarre figures of all sorts are found extensively in Southwestern rock art. The location of existing examples may provide evidence that the Indians were in or near a temporary camp or permanent settlement. There is also the possibility that the art in some cases could have had ceremonial or even calendrical significance along trade routes. This might explain why rock art appears in remote places which seem to have no other sign of habitation.

If a camp or village was established, it was a fairly simple matter to devise a calendar marker visible to anyone. Such an instrument would be desirable, since the group would need to know how to plan for hunting and planting, as well as for the all-important ceremonies to appease the gods and seek their favor.

Knowing the number of days until one of the solstices, a priest might easily make a marker for future reference by erecting a post. On the day of the solstice, the priest could then carefully trace the path of its shadow from sunrise to sunset.

If he chose, he could position other markers in the shadow's path, each with a designated ceremonial or religious meaning. Depending upon the terrain and available resources, he might instead pile stones where the shadow struck, or perhaps lay out a circle of stones.

While shadow projection was the primary means devised for tracking solstices, other markers were also used. An observer could place himself or another object in horizon alignment to a natural pillar in order to sight the rising and setting of the moon, Venus, Jupiter, Mars, the Pleiades and other heavenly bodies. This technique could be used on occasions when shadows would be weak or nonexistent.

Using the same principle, a stone circle could be arranged to represent the horizon. The observer would usually stand near the center, with selected stones at periodic intervals marking important horizon points.

Many stone circles of widely varying sizes have been found in North America. They were usually divided into four quadrants by a cross of stones to mark the four cardinal directions. Known as medicine wheels, many, but certainly not all of the circles, were designed as celestial observatories.

Today, they are sometimes constructed for ceremonial or religious purposes by individuals or groups seeking to return to the Native American belief systems as they have existed for the past several hundred years.

Interestingly, the same circle and cross design used for medicine wheels was also known to the Mesoamericans, and the design has been found in Teotihuacán. There, the cross corresponds to the celestial layout of the city. This symbol, whether employed as a medicine wheel or a petroglyph, has been found all over North America. Sometimes the petroglyphs consist only of a cross, leaving many contemporary viewers puzzling over the possibility of some pre-Columbian contact with Christianity.

Where large stone circles were constructed, their calendrical function could have been implemented either by horizon alignment or by erecting a post or stacking a pile of stones, if the shadow method was used. The design may have depended upon the observatory's purpose.

The essential data for marking the seasons was based on tracking the solstices. Once this was documented on location, it was a fairly simple matter to record the years as well as any important days within the 365 day solar year.

Accurate date keeping methods were vital for economic and religious purposes, and the knowledge of astronomy was carefully preserved through oral tradition, if not by more tangible means. The ancient science of skywatching was not hindered by the passing of years, cultural transitions, or the span of great distance.

A solstice or equinox, however, could also be documented by means other than circular observatories. For example, a shaman might simply erect a post to cast a shadow on or by a petroglyph such as a spiral or some other figure pecked into the rock. Painted pictographs could also substitute for petroglyphs. Obviously, after hundreds or even thousands of years, a wooden post would have left no trace, though the artwork might still remain.

Ancient skywatchers did not always rely on shadows or horizon alignments to indicate celestial events. The rays of the sun were also observed. With Anasazi architecture, windows in certain buildings such as ceremonial kivas, were occasionally positioned so that sunlight was directed to strike an object in the room.

In other instances, an opening may have been designed to allow sunlight to strike the opposite wall of the kiva sometime during the day of a solstice. This method was also employed by other cultures, including the Egyptians as well as the Indians of Mesoamerica.

One of the most fascinating prehistoric observatories in North America is the one in Chaco Canyon, New Mexico. High atop Fajada Butte, near the Anasazi ruins of Pueblo Bonito, is a remarkable solar calendar. Although researchers knew about the spiral petroglyphs at this site, their function was not discovered until 1977.

While resting by the large parallel stones at the location, artist Anna Sofaer witnessed the amazing operation of the calendar which continued to occur a few days after the summer solstice, though not with quite the same precision.

The solar device, also called a sun clock, includes a large and small spiral, each pecked into the surface of the rock wall. Massive stone slabs are turned edgewise and positioned vertically in front of the spirals. When the summer solstice occurs, a pointed shaft of light is thrown between the slabs creating a "sun dagger" that descends through the center of the large spiral. The spring or autumn equinox is indicated when a sun dagger simultaneously slices through each spiral. During the winter solstice, the large spiral is framed on each side by a dagger of light.

Further investigation has shown that this solar calendar, which probably dates to around A.D. 1100, also tracks a nineteen year lunar cycle using moonlight. At the time of its discovery, the Sun Dagger observatory was the only known device of its kind to have both solar and lunar functions.

Another extraordinary Anasazi calendar is located near Holly Ruin in Hovenweep National Monument, near the Colorado-Utah border. Under a rock overhang, two petroglyphs were positioned to indicate the summer solstice. At sunrise on June 21, narrow bands of horizontal light appear along the same plane with the spirals on the rock wall. Like arrows, the bands move toward each other to dissect the spirals through the center, then merge together in the middle. The process takes place in less than ten minutes.

It is impossible to tell what percentage of rock art may originally have had a functional connection with celestial phenomena, but certainly new discoveries will continue. Where a connection is suspected, the observer should look for at least two basic clues.

First, determine if the figures themselves seem to have any relationship to celestial figures associated with Mesoamerican religions. Second, look to see if the art is oriented to the eastern or western horizon. Remember that light or shadow markers may have long since disappeared.

Horizon alignments would also be a good indicator of celestial relationships, starting with the summer solstice (June 21, the longest day of the year); the autumn equinox (September 21); the winter solstice (December 21, the shortest day of the year); and the spring equinox (March 21). Observing the rising and setting of the moon, planets, stars and constellations would require a more detailed knowledge of directional orientation and celestial timetables.

Undoubtedly, there are still many examples of rock art with undocumented celestial functions. This is simply because they are often in remote places and observers are not on location at the right time to see the connection. Moreover, the discipline of archaeoastronomy is fairly new and not many individuals are familiar with the possibilities and what to look for.

As a rule, archaeologists have generally had a separate agenda, often considering rock art to be an indecipherable curiosity, though conceding that there may be religious or mythological meanings. Occasionally, it has simply been regarded as Indian graffiti. On the other hand, when a discovery contains something very unusual or significant, it may sometimes be concealed from the general public for fear of ignorant or malicious vandalism. Countless examples have already been lost forever.

The possibility of defacement or destruction is a legitimate concern, but hopefully students of archaeoastronomy will help to promote a greater public understanding and respect for these fragile and irreplaceable messages from the past.

## 5

## SACRIFICE ROCK

The phenomenon of Sacrifice Rock is unique. Nowhere else in the United States is there a natural rock configuration with such abundant possibilities relating to Native American traditions. Not only can the summer solstice be observed by the movement of a projected shadow, but also ancient religious and ceremonial associations seem clearly evident at the location.

The most extraordinary feature of Sacrifice Rock is the descending shadow figure which closely resembles the head of a howling coyote. The manifestation of the image is at first faint, almost imperceptibly emerging from the darkened desert varnish like the materialization of a spirit. The earliest observers, who began settling in Zion Canyon by A.D. 700, certainly must have believed the site held great mystical power.

Common to all the cultures of the Southwest is a crossover between the symbolism of religion and mythology, probably a result of storytelling and secular interpretation of religious themes. Nonetheless, even though many symbols have acquired multiple meanings over several thousand

*Anasazi Sunrise*

years, there are still significant similarities between the ancient religions of Mesoamerica and North America which transcend both time and distance. The petroglyphs at Sacrifice Rock are an illustration of this principle.

### COYOTE

At the base of the group of petroglyphs pecked in the panel is a small wolf or dog-like figure. It may represent a coyote, since the figure could also indicate the rock's connection with the howling shadow image, providing identification to travelers or those making a pilgrimage to the site. Moreover, it probably served in the ceremonial rituals normally observed on the occasion of a solstice.

The coyote has played a significant role in American Indian religion and mythology since very early times. He appears in creation accounts and is often associated with the sun and stars. In the mythology, the coyote eventually assumed the role of the Trickster, who had a penchant for working mischief among humans as well as in the heavens.

50

## PHALLUS

Just below the area on the megalith where the coyote shadow first appears is a life-size phallic petroglyph. This symbol has classically been associated with regeneration and resurrection--concepts that are consistent with the ancient fertility rites celebrated at solstice observances the world over. Death and rebirth were symbolized by sunset and sunrise wherever the sun was worshipped.

## SPIRAL

The central petroglyph at Sacrifice Rock is the spiral, most important because of its relationship to the coyote shadow during the summer solstice. The spiral itself may represent the sun, which seems consistent with other examples of rock art. The spiral is certainly the symbol of choice for the sun calendars in Hovenweep and Chaco Canyon. There is a strong probability that the spirals found in these locations may also represent the serpent.

Snake images, including flying serpents and feathered serpents, are common in Southwestern rock art. Indeed, the seemingly abstract design the observer perceives as a spiral may more realistically be the graphic image of a coiled snake. The similarity is especially apparent at Chaco Canyon where the smaller of the two spirals is partially uncoiled.

The Feathered Serpent deity can be traced through Mesoamerican religions at least since the Olmec civilization, dating to 1000 B.C. This god, along with other celestial deities, was worshipped until the collapse of the Aztec empire. The Feathered Serpent was know as Quetzalcóatl among the Nahuatl-speaking Aztecs. They believed that he and his companion, Xólotl, the dog-headed god, created mankind in the fifth and present creation. Quetzalcóatl was also identified with Venus (the Morning and Evening star) and had the power of death and resurrection.

Another interesting association between the sun and the serpent is seen on the Temple of Quetzalcóatl at Teotihuacán. Carved into that structure is the image of the Fire Serpent, which carried the sun on its back on its daily journey across the heavens.

For the Anasazi, perhaps time and culture developed the convention of depicting the serpent more often in a coiled position, which could also serve to symbolize the disc of the sun. If the symbol has its origin in the Feathered Serpent deity, practicality might dictate the need to drop the embellishment of feathers when the petroglyph was fashioned as a spiral form. The shape is certainly more useful in conjunction with the light or shadow projection which pierces or splits the spiral during the solstice phenomenon at Chaco Canyon, Hovenweep National Monument, and Zion.

## CIRCLE AND DOT

Slightly above and to the right of the spiral at Sacrifice Rock is a circle with a dot in the center. During the summer solstice, the coyote shadow does not approach this symbol. Its function is still uncertain, and will require further study and observation. Perhaps it represents the moon, or even water.

When explaining rock art elsewhere, some contemporary American Indians contend that this symbol represents the sun, with the central dot signifying a life- sustaining umbilical cord. The same symbol, however, can be traced to the Mayas, who depicted Venus with a similar image. Venus may be the better explanation for this glyph at Sacrifice Rock, especially since Venus portrays death and resurrection, and was also identified with the Feathered Serpent. Moreover, it would seem logical to use this setting as the ideal station to observe the rising planet. A glyph to that effect would therefore be appropriate.

## EAGLE FEET

There are three pairs of eagle feet petroglyphs on the panel. Two of them are positioned to interact with the downward progression of the coyote shadow at the summer solstice. The first instance occurs when the shadow simultaneously frames the foot farthest to the left, the spiral, and the dog-coyote glyph.

The second instance occurs when the nose of the shadow seems to pivot around to the bottom of the lowermost eagle foot. Perhaps significantly, by the time the shadow has descended to this point, there is no longer much resemblance to the coyote. Instead, an ancient observer having an imagination already charged with thoughts of the supernatural might easily perceive the image's transformation into the outstretched wing of an eagle.

The eagle and the sun are closely associated in Mesoamerican sun worship. Eagles (along with the serpent and coyote) are depicted on the

Temple of the Sun at Teotihuacán.  The Aztec calendar, which is based on the Mayan calendar, portrays Tonatiuh the sun god framed on each side by eagle claws grasping human hearts.  The Aztec religion also linked the eagle with the rising and setting of the sun.

The eagle-sun connection remains intact even in contemporary Native American religion.  The Sun Dance ceremony, practiced by the Plains Indians in modern times, illustrates the likelihood that it is rooted in the ancient religions of Mexico and Central America.  In his book, THE SPIRITUAL LEGACY OF THE AMERICAN INDIAN, Joseph Epes Brown describes significant aspects of the Sun Dance:

*To construct from timbers brought from the mountains the circular ceremonial lodge, the lodge of "new birth," "new life," the "thirst lodge," is to reenact the creation of world and cosmos. Horizontally, the lodge doorway situated in the east is the place whence flows life in light; from the south comes growth in youth, from the west ripeness, full fruit, and middle age, and from the north completion and old age leading to death, which leads again to new life.  At the center of the lodge the most sacred cottonwood tree, rooted in the womb of mother earth and stretching up and out to the heavens, is the axis of the world and the male generative principle. Into and out of this central point and axis of the lodge flow the powers of the six directions. When men in awful ceremony are actually tied to this Tree of Center with the flesh of their bodies, or when women make offerings of pieces of flesh cut from their arms, sacrifice through suffering is accomplished that the world and all beings may live, that life may be renewed, that human beings may realize their identity (Brown, pp. 102-103).*

Pain, suffering and the shedding of blood provide  propitiation to the sacred powers, enabling men to assume the spirit of the eagle and achieve unification with the sun itself:

*Dancers wear and use whistles made of the wing-bone of an eagle to which eagle plumes are attached. In recreating the cry of the eagle in the powerful rhythm of song, dance, and drum, the eagle is present in voice and being; a human being's vital breath is united with the essence of the sun and life. Through such ritual use of sacred form a human becomes an eagle, and the eagle with its plumes is the sun (Brown, p. 104).*

The Sun Dance is usually performed on or near the day of the summer solstice, a celestial event which itself has been symbolic of the renewal of life in the ancient religions. Thus, in contrast to the Western view of time and life which is perceived to be linear, Native Americans have sustained a cyclical view of time, life and reality. This is epitomized by the cycles of the sun and the flourishing life of summer.

*The Sun Dance is not a celebration by humans for humans; it is an honoring of all life and the source of all life that life may continue, that the circle be a cycle, that all the world and humankind may continue on the path of the cycle of giving, receiving, bearing, being born in suffering, growing, becoming, returning to the earth that which has been given, and finally being born again. Only in sacrifice is sacredness accomplished; only in sacrifice is identity found. It is only through suffering in sacrifice that freedom is finally known and laughter in joy returns to the world (Brown, p.105).†*

The Sun Dance as we know it today is a relatively modern ceremony, yet the essence of its religious themes have prevailed throughout time. It may well be that some of the ritual ceremonies practiced at Sacrifice Rock and other sacred observatories were germane to the early development of the North American Indian's traditional heritage.

## THE SETTING

The configuration of the  stones at Sacrifice Rock should not be overlooked.  The overall setting may have had considerable significance within the context of the Anasazi religion.  In the first place, the stones are located near the apex of two slopes that combine to form a natural amphitheater.  While the megalith itself functioned like  a  projection screen, it may also have served as a sounding board to help amplify the words and chants of a priest or shaman.

## PLATFORM STONE

Just a few feet in front, and a little to the left, of the megalith is a large flattened boulder which would make an ideal platform on which to stand while presiding over ceremonial rites.

Standing atop the boulder, bathed in full sunlight, a man would be clearly visible to a large crowd.  The coyote shadow image and brightly lit panel would loom behind him.  Because of the angle of the sun, however, his own shadow would fall on the ground to the left and away from the megalith.

The panel may have been further embellished with pictographs drawn in charcoal, mineral- or vegetable-base paints long since weathered away.

## EMERGENCE PASSAGE

To the right and through the center of the stones which support the inverted V-shaped, shadow wedge is a narrow tunnel perhaps twelve or fifteen feet long.  It is just large enough for a crouching man to pass through.

Mesoamerican and Southwestern Indian cosmologies share the common view that mankind originated from the underworld, emerging from the womb of mother earth.  The natural passage at Sacrifice Rock could have provided an excellent facility for early ceremonial reenactments of the tradition.  This belief, which also symbolized new birth, remained strong in the Anasazi culture. In later developmental periods it was represented by a hole in the kiva floor called a "sipapu."  The tradition is still maintained by the present-day Hopi Indians.

## ALTAR STONE

Slightly forward, between the mouth of the "emergence passage" and the platform stone, is a massive, almost cube-shaped block, oddly resembling an altar. On its top is a concave depression roughly 1½ by 3 feet across. It appears to collect and hold rain water, and there are signs of water stains down its face from the overflow. Could this depression have been used as a catch basin for blood? Admittedly, such a possibility is only an inference, based on incomplete evidence. Nonetheless, its shape, placement, and association with the other formations and symbols certainly leads to some interesting speculation.

Self-mutilation and bloodletting were common to the religious systems of pre-Columbian America. Human blood was often drawn before and during ceremonies, as well as in preparation for various sacrifices. Blood was believed to provide nourishment for the sun as well as for mother earth, and was usually obtained by piercing or cutting an ear, the tongue, lips or penis. Animals were also offered, but human sacrifice increased in frequency until it became the primary form of offering among the Aztecs.

The Anasazi, however, left no written records, murals, sculptures or depictions on pottery that clearly indicate they may have engaged in sacrificing humans to the sun or some other deity. Current archaeological indications, along with the apparent culture and economy of the Anasazi, seem to argue against such practice. The shedding of blood, however, was an integral part of sun worship, and the possibility of bloodletting or limited human sacrifice cannot be ruled out entirely.

Human sacrifice commonly occurred throughout Mesoamerica and was regularly employed by the Mississippians, probably as late as the arrival of Columbus. However, it was the Aztecs, preying mostly on their enemies, who carried the macabre rite to its extreme. Removing the beating hearts from their victims, they made hundreds of thousands of offerings to the sun during their relatively brief reign. It has even been suggested that a protein shortage in their diet led to the development of ritual cannibalism.

Several methods of inflicting death were used by the various Indian cultures to appease their gods, including arrow shooting, beheading and strangulation. But if a tribal group sacrificed one of its own members, it was usually considered an honor to be chosen. The victim often submitted willingly, though sometimes with the aid of an anesthetizing drug.

The science of celestial observation among the pre-Columbian Indians was a vital component of their religion. The Anasazi shared many of the major doctrines common throughout the Americas during prehistoric times. Though the names and appearances of the major deities among cultures often differed, their function in the supernatural world and their demands for propitiation were very similar.

The Virgin Anasazi lived and traveled along the Virgin River for over a thousand years between 100 B.C. and A.D. 1100. Could Sacrifice Rock indeed have been used as a site for some type of ritual human sacrifice? The answer to that question remains a mystery.

The monumental stones are not far from the Virgin River, and a nearby village surely would have been close to the riverbank. Notwithstanding, the high water and flash flood potential over the last 1200 years or longer may explain why so little evidence about the local inhabitants remains if a village did indeed exist there. Perhaps buried under the silt deposits or beneath the fill washed down from the canyon walls, another clue lies waiting.

† THE SPIRITUAL LEGACY OF THE AMERICAN INDIAN
by Joseph Epes Brown
Copyright © 1982 by Joseph Epes Brown
Reprinted by permission of the Crossroad Publishing Company

**The Howling Coyote Appears**
Dr. Charles McDowell          Dr. Stephen Preacher

The Descent Begins

Framing the Glyphs

Splitting the Spiral

"Eagle Wing"

The preceeding photographs were taken by Ronda Preacher on June 21, 1991. They are the first photos ever taken of the solstice phenomenon at Sacrifice Rock.

# 6

## FLASHBACK

Still cloaked in the gray shadow of the east canyon rim, the sacred stone stood waiting silently, like a sentinel on duty. It had witnessed the ascension of Tonatiuh, the sun god, for years beyond counting.

Totepzin, the high priest, peered out expectantly over the gathering villagers as their line snaked toward him in quiet reverence. It was but a few hundred reed lengths to walk from the simple village by the river. Wisps of smoke from the morning fires were gently wafted away by the gathering morning breezes.

The distant wailing of an infant reached Totepzin's ears and he winced as it jarred the mood of his meditation. Undaunted, the People continued to make their way up the gradually rising slope of the canyon floor, assembling in the natural amphitheater which embraced the sacred megalith. Their demeanor was that of passive resignation knowing that, in exchange for the hope of a fruitful season, they must offer Kulna, the eldest daughter of Chichéma, the village's most skilled basketmaker. But their sadness would last only a short time. Her spirit would soon rise on eagle wings to meet the sun, and then the village would rejoice with celebration and feasting. Tonatiuh would surely be pleased and shine down his blessing.

Totepzin shivered. He had not slept or eaten for two nights. The sweat of anticipation chilled his blood-streaked chest and arms as Ehécatl, the wind spirit, breathed on him. Most of the precious ceremonial oil he had rubbed on himself had since been drunken by his thirsty skin, but its strong musky fragrance gave him strength. After a long night of prayer and chanting, his throat was parched. He reached for the gourd which held the brew of fermented corn mixed with turkey blood. The throbbing from his lanced ear lobes could now be eased, and he drank deeply.

It would not be much longer. Tonatiuh's rays were sliding down the west canyon wall, igniting the rimrocks in flaming light. He knew that the top of the massive stone would soon begin to catch those rays even while the ground around him still remained in shadow. Then, Coyote would return. Coyote, who was called Xólotl, brother to Quetzalcóatl, the Feathered Serpent. Together, they had recreated man on the dawn of the fifth creation, when the world was once again made new.

Totepzin trembled as he reflected on his privilege to conduct this sacred ceremony. The People believed he had inherited great power, and all his life his father instructed him in the ways of the spirit world. Once again he remembered the story his grandfather told him many times as a child. It was his own grandfather who had first seen the manifestation of Xólotl, the coyote-headed god.

Grandfather had been seeking a special stone to serve as a permanent indicator for the day of regeneration, the longest day of the year. The sacred knowledge of the heavens had been passed down to him from his ancestors who came to dwell among the People long ago--priests who had once lived in the rich and distant land to the south. In that land, he was told, the people outnumbered the stars and lived in cities with great avenues and magnificent temples rising up to the sun.

The wizened priest scoured the canyon many times for the best location. The People needed a calendar not only to tell the season for planting, but also to mark the times for hunting, the performance of the rain rituals, and the other important ceremonies they must hold. But most of all, they needed a sacred altar upon which they could thank Tonatiuh for his blessings and pray for renewed prosperity. Tonatiuh brought life each day. An offering of blood would provide him nourishment, giving him strength to protect the People from the wrath of the other gods.

The old man looked for a flat, east-facing stone where Tonatiuh would cause a shadow to fall on the solstice day. Then, as the rising orb pushed the shadow across the rock's face, he could trace its movement with charcoal. His next task would be to etch the surface, carefully pecking away the dark coating to reveal the living rock underneath. The spirits would tell him what image to make. Perhaps it would be the essence of an ancestor. With the right stone, the images could last for all who came after him. He paused to pray for guidance.

Totepzin's grandfather had stopped to wait by the strange megalith, hoping the large angular slab before it would throw a shadow on the smooth and beautiful panel. Was the alignment correct? Or would it already be too low by the time Tonatiuh rose in rebirth from the underworld? He waited patiently. If this place was right, the People could make their new camp between this mighty guardian and the life-sustaining river nearby.

How would the ancient rock catch the sun's first rays? While he mused, staring at the rich brown shades of the stone's face, it suddenly began to glow as light beams flashed over the eastern rim of the canyon. Well above his height, the dark shading along the left edge of the flat surface intensified.

Suddenly, as the contrasting light grew stronger, the shape of a coyote's head materialized, its nose pointing due north. He stared in apprehension as the howling image began to move slowly down the face of the panel, until at last it was within reach. With a charred twig, he marked its progress, carefully outlining the shadow's dimensions at successive stages.

At about shoulder level, Grandfather sketched a coiled serpent, its dimensions exactly matching the width of the shadow's snout. His hand shook with excitement as he realized the Sun Father had chosen him to witness the celestial revelation of Coyote's spirit image. Nowhere in the memory of his people had anyone seen such a wonder. He would become a great and revered priest in the eyes of all generations to follow.

Leaving those reflections, Totepzin knew the power of Grandfather's spirit still lived within his breast. He licked the salty sweat above his lip and stepped up onto the flat round boulder that would serve as his platform. From this position he would conduct the ceremony of renewal and unification once again. Standing in front of the panel and near the base of the shadow wedge, he could be clearly seen by all the People. Bathed in the brilliant light, the megalith close behind him made his words and chants stronger, yet his own shadow would not interfere with Coyote's spirit image.

He untied the sheepskin pouch he wore at his waist and placed it near his feet. First with his right hand, then his left, he reached inside filling each fist with corn. Arms upraised, he began chanting a prayer to the Creator. Then slowly lowering his arms in great arcs, his pitch changed to a lower, throaty chant to the Earth Mother. Modulating his pitch yet again, he stretched his arms to the north, east, south and west, completing the entire circle of the Four Directions. When he was finished, he extended the fingers of his up-turned palms, allowing the grains of corn to fall to the earth as a thank offering.

Just at that moment, Tonatiuh's rays struck the top of the megalith. A sudden stillness fell over the People, and they prayed that Coyote, the spirit image of Xólotl, would again return. Last year the Sun Father had hidden his face behind brooding clouds, for he was not pleased. That was a bad omen and the last growing season had been short, and the rain scarce. Frost time came early and the coldness bit deeply. With little food, many grandmothers had died. This time it would be better. Within a few more breaths, Coyote would surely appear to witness their precious offering.

The high priest stood ready, his tortoise shell rattle in hand. Shafts of light broke over the eastern rim, forcing him to squint in the glare. Glancing around at the panel, he saw the spirit image faintly begin to emerge. Overhead, an eagle's scream suddenly pierced the hushed silence, sending icy fingers of awe down his spine. A gasp of astonishment rose in unison from the crowd below him.

Kulna looked up, her face radiant with joy. She now knew her journey would be without fear. It would not be long before she would soar as one of the Quauhteca, the Eagle People.

Once again, Totepzin began to chant, shaking the rattle in rhythm with his speeding heart. Tonatiuh, the sun god, would soon be satisfied.

## 7

## PROTECTION AND PRESERVATION

Sacrifice Rock stands like an enigma in Zion Canyon. The interpretation of events and circumstances surrounding the observatory will probably remain controversial. From that controversy, however, may arise a greater appreciation for the complex Anasazi culture--a culture which has not only left many unanswered questions, but also which continues to present new ones.

Much information about ancient American civilization has been lost forever, but what remains should not be taken for granted. Indeed, the simple, seemingly crude symbols on the face of Sacrifice Rock have finally provided the first piece of an intricate puzzle. But the puzzle will not be complete until many more questions about the Anasazi are answered, and many more celestial observations are made.

There is yet much to learn. For example, where does the shadow fall during the winter solstice? What effect may be seen on the days of the spring and autumn equinoxes? Do shadow patterns interact with the petroglyphs during a moonrise? How might the alignments of other celestial bodies such as Venus and the Pleiades be involved?

Long after these questions are finally answered, people will still be drawn to Sacrifice Rock. They will come to marvel at the inventiveness of prehistoric man working in concert with the rhythms of nature, and to wonder at the phenomena which sparked his imagination.

Before making this discovery public, I informed a small handful of National Park Service officials about the existence of Zion's sun clock. It is very fortunate that this marvelous timepiece lies within easy surveillance of the park rangers, but they cannot be on site at all times. More remains to be done to help ensure its protection, and this will require the interest and help of all visitors to the site.

Most importantly, the vandalism must be stopped. Although defacement and destruction of antiquities within the National Park system is a Federal offense, many vandals are ignorant of the laws, or simply don't care. Any one witnessing vandalism should report it to the park rangers.

The fragile nature of the stones is another serious concern. The panel is showing evidence of encroaching exfoliation from moisture absorption at its base. Although the process is natural, it will eventually cause the petroglyphs to peel away from the megalith if preventive measures are not taken. Some loss already may have occurred. A careful study of methods to stabilize the glyphs should be undertaken. In addition, the shadow wedge itself is in danger of damage. While it has endured for perhaps thousands of years in its present condition, it is no match for the abuse of people climbing all over its delicate tip--the portion responsible for the marvelous coyote image.

Before the wonder of Sacrifice Rock is lost to future generations, authorized individuals should take careful measurements and document all aspects of the configuration. In the event of further destruction, natural or otherwise, the data would then be available to undertake restoration. In the meantime, park visitors should be informed about the importance of this great antiquity. Efforts to restore the panel from existing defacement should also begin.

Protecting Sacrifice Rock will require vigilance from government officials, the Park Service, and finally, from each visitor who seeks the opportunity to enjoy the ancient observatory and wonder at the role it may have played in our Native American heritage.

# SELECTED BIBLIOGRAPHY

AMERICA'S FASCINATING INDIAN HERITAGE. Editors of The Reader's Digest Association. Pleasantville: Reader's Digest Association, 1990.

Bahti, Tom. SOUTHWESTERN INDIAN CEREMONIALS. Las Vegas: K.C. Publications, 1970.

Barnes, F. A. CANYON COUNTRY PREHISTORIC ROCK ART. Salt Lake City: Wasatch Publishers, 1982.

Brown, Joseph Epes. SPIRITUAL LEGACY OF THE AMERICAN INDIANS. New York: Crossroad Publishing Co., 1985.

Bushnell, G. H. S. ANCIENT ARTS OF THE AMERICAS. Villalongin, Mexico: Ediciiones Lara, 1967.

Canby, Thomas Y. "The Anasazi, Riddles in the Ruins." in *National Geographic*. Vol. 162, No. 5. Washington, D.C.: National Geographic Society, October, 1982

Carlson, John B. "America's Ancient Skywatchers," in *National Geographic*. Vol. 177, No. 3. Washington, D. C.: National Geographic Society, March, 1990.

Cirlot, J.E. A DICTIONARY OF SYMBOLS. Oxford, Great Britain: Alden Press, 1962.

Creamer, Winifred and Jonathan Haas. "Pueblo," in *National Geographic*. Vol. 180, No. 4. Washington, D. C.: National Geographic Society, October, 1991.

Davies, Nigel. THE TOLTECS UNTIL THE FALL OF TULA. Norman: University of Oklahoma Press. 1977.

89

Davies, Nigel. THE TOLTEC HERITAGE. Norman: University of Oklahoma Press, 1980.

Erdoes, Richard, and Alfonso Ortiz, editors. AMERICAN INDIANS: MYTHS AND LEGENDS. New York: Pantheon Books, 1984.

Ferguson, William M., and Arthur H. Rohn. ANASAZI RUINS OF THE SOUTHWEST IN COLOR. Albuquerque: University of New Mexico Press, 1991.

Hultkrantz, Ake. THE RELIGIONS OF THE AMERICAN INDIANS. Berkeley: University of California Press, 1967.

Lamb, Wendell, and Lawrence W. Shultz. INDIAN LORE. Winona Lake: Light and Life Press, 1964.

Leonard, Jonathan Norton, and Editors of Time-Life Books. ANCIENT AMERICA. New York: Time Incorporated.

Lister, Robert H. and Florence C. Lister. THOSE WHO CAME BEFORE. Tucson: University of Arizona Press, 1983.

Martin, Paul S., and George I. Quimby, and Donald Collier. INDIANS BEFORE COLUMBUS. Chicago: University of Chicago Press, 1949.

Muench, David, and Donald G. Pike. ANASAZI: ANCIENT PEOPLE OF THE ROCK. Palo Alto: America West Publishing Company, 1974.

"Native American Heritage: A Visitor's Guide." Supplement to the National Geographic Magazine, Vol. 180, No. 4. Washington, D. C.: National Geographic Society, October, 1991.

Noble, David Grant. ANCIENT RUINS OF THE SOUTHWEST. Flagstaff: Northland Press, 1981.

Schaafsma, Polly. INDIAN ROCK ART OF THE SOUTHWEST. Albuquerque: University of New Mexico Press, 1980.

Stokes, William Michael, and William Lee Stokes. MESSAGES ON STONE. Salt Lake City: Starstone Publishing Company, 1980.

Strong, Emory. STONE AGE IN THE GREAT BASIN. Portland: Binfords and Mort, Publishers, 1969.

Stuart, George E. "Etowah," in *National Geographic*. Vol. 180, No. 4. Washington, D. C.: National Geographic Society, October, 1991.

Sun Bear (Chippewa Indian), Wabun Wind, and Chrysalis Mulligan. DANCING WITH THE WHEEL: THE MEDICINE WHEEL WORKBOOK. New York: Prentice Hall Press, 1991.

Vaillant, G. C. AZTECS OF MEXICO. Baltimore: Doubleday and Company, 1968.

Waters, Frank. THE BOOK OF THE HOPI. New York: Ballantine Books, 1969.

Williamson, Ray A., Howard H. Fisher, and Donnel O'Flynn. "Anasazi Solar Observations," in NATIVE AMERICAN ASTRONOMY, ed. by Anthony F. Aveni. Austin: University of Texas Press, 1977.

Wilson, Josleen. THE PASSIONATE AMATEUR'S GUIDE TO ARCHAEOLOGY IN THE UNITED STATES. New York: Macmillan Publishing Co., 1980.

## THE AUTHOR

Dr. Stephen Preacher has maintained an interest in Native Americans most of his life. He is the academic vice-president of Christian Heritage College, in El Cajon, California, where he resides with his wife and children.

# ANASAZI SUNRISE™ T-shirts!

Express your individuality while helping to promote an awareness and understanding of Sacrifice Rock -- the Secret of the Anasazi Indians. Wear the distinctive turquoise Coyote Shadow with the yellow Sunrise Spiral. A terrific conversation piece! All Tees are high quality white HANES 50-50 shirts, made in the USA.

☐ Please send me _____ ANASAZI SUNRISE™ T-shirts for only $11.95 each.
Check desired sub-caption:

☐ "The Mystery of Sacrifice Rock"
Qty _____ Size(s) _____

☐ "I Saw the Shadow"
Qty _____ Size(s) _____

Adult M, L, XL, XXL
Youth S, M, L

Mail this coupon, or a photocopy, to:

**The Rugged Individualist**
Box 2565  El Cajon, CA  92019

Your satisfaction guaranteed or we will gladly refund or exchange your purchase. Please allow 2-4 weeks for delivery.

☐ Please send me _____ copy(s) of the book,
ANASAZI SUNRISE @ $6.95 each.

☐ Please send me more information about unique products available from **The Rugged Individualist.**

Your Name _____

Street _____

City _____ State _____ Zip _____

I have enclosed a check or money order for:

$ _____ sub-total
$ _____ (Tax -CA residents only)
$ 2.2 5 Shipping and handling
$ _____ Total amount enclosed